"There are no ordinary people. You have never talked to a mere mortal," wrote C. S. Lewis. It's true—each one of us is a special creation of God.

Believe it or not—no one else is just like you. Your physical appearance, your voice and personality traits—your habits, intelligence, personal tastes—all these make you one of a kind. Even your fingerprints distinguish you from every other human being—past, present, or future. You are not the product of some cosmic assembly line; you are unique.

But the most important fact of your identity is that God created you in his own image (Genesis 1:27). He made you so you could share in his creation, could love and laugh and know him person to person. You are special indeed!

The Bible reveals God's total interest in you as an individual. The psalmist wrote in one of his most beautiful prayers, "I praise you, for I am fearfully and wonderfully made" (Psalm 139:14). God knew

The Lord your God is in your midst, a mighty one who will save; he will rejoice over you with gladness; he will quiet you by his love; he will exult over you with loud singing.

ZEPHANIAH 3:17

CROSSWAY

The Lord Jesus saves all who believe in him.
To learn more about Jesus as Lord and Savior visit ESV.org/Jesus.

O God, I believe that Jesus Christ is your Son, and that you have opened the eyes of my heart to see the truth of Christ and my great need for him. I see that I am a sinner and need forgiveness. I see that Christ died for sinners and rose again. I see the wonderful promise that all who believe in Christ receive this forgiveness and eternal life. So I do believe, and I appeal to your mercy to save me from my sin, and welcome me, as you promised, into eternal life with you. Put your Spirit within me, I pray, and give me all the help I need to follow Jesus as Lord, and obey his teachings. Please lead me to a Bible-believing church where I can grow in faith and with others who love Jesus. Amen.

© 2019 by John Piper. Published by Crossway.

CROSSWAY

GOOD NEWS *Tracts*

9 781682 164037

www.goodnewstracts.org